Shaquille O'Neal

by Bob Woods

Troll Associates

Library of Congress Cataloging-in-Publication Data
Woods, Bob
Shaquille O'Neal / by Bob Woods
p.   cm.
ISBN 0-8167-3568-9
1. O'Neal, Shaquille—Juvenile literature.
2. Basketball players—United States—Biography—Juvenile literature.   I. Title
GV884.054W66   1995   796.323'092—dc20   [B]   94-22752

Cover Photo: Focus on Sports
Interior Photo Credits: Page 1: Tim O'Dell/Sports Illustrated; Page 3: Manny Millan/Sports Illustrated; Page 5, 7: Focus on Sports; Page 9: Jerry Wachter/Focus on Sports; Page 11, 19, 25, 32: Bill Frakes/Sports Illustrated; Page 13: Lou Cappozolo/Sports Illustrated; Page 15, 17: David Klutho/Sports Illustrated; Page 21, 27, 29, 31: AP/Wide World Photos; Page 23: John McDonough/Sports Illustrated.
Designed by Antler & Baldwin, Inc.

(B)asketball player Shaquille O'Neal is a big star in more ways than one. "Shaq," as he is known by millions of fans, is 7-feet, 1-inch tall and weighs 303 pounds. He towers over most other players. Shaq is also a big man in terms of popularity. He's one of the most famous athletes in the world.

Shaquille is the All-Star center for the Orlando Magic of the National Basketball Association (NBA). He was also a star of Dream Team II, which won the 1994 World Championship in Toronto, Canada. Shaq played so well in those games that he was named MVP (Most Valuable Player). But life was not always so magical for the big man.

Shaq was born on March 6, 1972, in a poor neighborhood in Newark, New Jersey. Kids teased Shaquille because of his big size and his unusual name, which means "little warrior" in Arabic. Sometimes young Shaquille got into fights. But his dad, Philip Harrison, taught him that becoming an athlete was a better way to prove himself.

Shaquille's dad was a sergeant in the U.S. Army. He moved the family to a military base in Germany when Shaq was 10. That's when Shaquille started playing football, baseball, and basketball, which became his favorite sport. He was big, clumsy, and not very good at first, but he worked hard to get better.

By age 13, Shaquille was already 6-feet, 5-inches tall. He wore a gigantic size 17 sneaker. Despite his size, Shaq was not good enough to make his school's basketball team. Still, he kept practicing and working out with his dad. "I learned never to give up," Shaquille recalls.

In 1987, when Shaq was 15, he and his family moved back to the United States. They lived on an army base in San Antonio, Texas. Shaq had improved a lot as a basketball player. He could dunk the ball, jump high for rebounds, and block shots. He became the star of the basketball team at Robert G. Cole High School. Shaquille wore number 33 in honor of his idol—Kareem Abdul-Jabbar, the sensational center for the Los Angeles Lakers.

Shaquille was 7-feet tall in his senior year of high school. He averaged 32 points, 22 rebounds, and 8 blocked shots in his last year at Cole High. More than 100 colleges offered Shaq basketball scholarships. He finally chose Louisiana State University (LSU) in Baton Rouge. He played so well during his first year in college that he made the freshman All-America team. He was also a solid B student in the classroom.

Shaquille was awesome in his second year at LSU. In a big game against the University of Arizona Wildcats, Shaq led the LSU Tigers to a 92-82 victory. He scored 24 points, grabbed 14 rebounds, and blocked shots. Later that season, Shaquille scored 33 points in a game against the University of Kentucky. Afterward, the Kentucky coach said, "He's simply the best college player in America."

Shaquille thought about leaving college after his sensational sopho-more season to become a pro basketball player. But after talking with his parents and coaches, he decided to stay at LSU. "Education, that's the main thing," said his father.

By his junior year in college, Shaq had grown to 7-feet, 1-inch. That year Shaq powered the LSU Tigers to a 21-10 record. He led the nation with 5.2 blocked shots per game.

On June 24, 1992, Shaquille was the first player chosen in the NBA draft. He was picked by the Orlando Magic, which plays its home games near Disney World in Florida. The 20-year-old rookie had a fantastic season. In a game against Michael Jordan and the world champion Chicago Bulls, Shaq scored 31 points, pulled down 24 rebounds, and blocked 5 shots. Thanks to Shaq, the Magic beat the Bulls.

Shaquille was chosen to be the starting center in the 1993 All-Star Game. It was a great honor for a first-year player. His teammates in that game were some of basketball's greatest superstars, including Charles Barkley of the Phoenix Suns, Hakeem Olajuwon of the Houston Rockets, and Patrick Ewing of the New York Knicks. By the end of his first season as a pro, Shaq was so terrific that he was voted the NBA Rookie of the Year.

Playing basketball is not the only thing Shaquille likes to do. He enjoys spending free time at his mansion outside of Orlando with his parents and two younger sisters, Lateefah and Ayesha, and his little brother, Jamal. And he loves playing video games with teammates Anfernee Hardaway and Dennis Scott. Shaq has also recorded his own rap-music album, written a book about his life, and starred in the movie *Blue Chips.*

As a pro, Shaquille earned the nickname "Shaq Attack." In his second season, 1993-94, he was one of the NBA's best players. He scored 53 points in a game against the Minnesota Timberwolves. It was the most points ever for an Orlando player.

Shaq is famous for his monster slam-dunks. One dunk was so powerful it tore the hoop from the backboard!

Shaq is so tall, quick, and strong that when he catches the ball near the hoop, he can slam-dunk over most players almost every time. Still, Shaquille is always working to become a better jump shooter and foul shooter.

In 1994 Shaquille led the Magic to the playoffs for the first time. He played well in the first round against Reggie Miller and the Indiana Pacers, but Orlando lost three games in a row. After the season, Shaq went back to LSU during the summer to finish getting his college degree. So now Shaq has one more very important reason to be proud of himself.

Full Name: Shaquille Rashaun O'Neal
Position: Center, Orlando Magic
Number: 32
College: Louisiana State University
Born: March 6, 1972; Newark, New Jersey
Home: Lake Butler, Florida
Hobbies: Acting, rap music, video games, karate
Favorite Food: Macaroni and cheese